BASEBALL LEGENDS

Hank Aaron
Grover Cleveland Alexander
Ernie Banks
Johnny Bench
Yogi Berra
Roy Campanella
Roberto Clemente
Ty Cobb
Dizzy Dean
Joe DiMaggio
Bob Feller
Jimmie Foxx
Lou Gehrig
Bob Gibson
Rogers Hornsby
Reggie Jackson
Shoeless Joe Jackson
Walter Johnson
Sandy Koufax
Mickey Mantle
Christy Mathewson
Willie Mays
Stan Musial
Satchel Paige
Brooks Robinson
Frank Robinson
Jackie Robinson
Pete Rose
Babe Ruth
Nolan Ryan
Mike Schmidt
Tom Seaver
Duke Snider
Warren Spahn
Willie Stargell
Casey Stengel
Honus Wagner
Ted Williams
Carl Yastrzemski
Cy Young

NEWFIELD
PUBLICATIONS

BASEBALL LEGENDS

DIZZY DEAN

Jack Kavanagh

Introduction by
Jim Murray

Senior Consultant
Earl Weaver

CHELSEA HOUSE PUBLISHERS
New York • Philadelphia

Published by arrangement with
Chelsea House Publishers.
Newfield Publications is a federally
registered trademark of Newfield
Publications, Inc.

Produced by James Charlton Associates
New York, New York.

Designed by Hudson Studio
Ossining, New York.

Typesetting by LinoGraphics
New York, New York.

Picture research by Carolann Hawkins
Cover illustration by Dan O'Leary

Library of Congress Cataloging-in-Publication Data

Kavanagh, Jack.
    Dizzy Dean / Jack Kavanagh ; introduction by Jim Murray.
p. cm.—(Baseball legends)
Includes bibliographical references.
    Summary: Follows the life of the man who, in his prime, led major
league baseball in wins, strikeouts, complete games, and innings
pitched and moved on to a broadcasting career after his retirement
as a player.
ISBN 0-7910-1173-9.—ISBN 0-7910-1207-7 (pbk.)
1. Dean, Dizzy, 1911-1974—Juvenile literature. 2. Baseball
players—United States—Biography—Juvenile literature. 3. Baseball
players. [1. Dean, Dizzy, 1911-1974.] I. Title. II. Series.
GV865.D4K38 1990
92—dc20   90-35387
[796.357'092]   CIP
[B]   AC

CONTENTS

WHAT MAKES A STAR

Jim Murray

No one has ever been able to explain to me the mysterious alchemy that makes one man a .350 hitter and another player, more or less identical in physical makeup, hard put to hit .200. You look at an Al Kaline, who played with the Detroit Tigers from 1953 to 1974. He was pale, stringy, almost poetic-looking. He always seemed to be struggling against a bad case of mononucleosis. But with a bat in his hands, he was King Kong. During his career, he hit 399 home runs, rapped out 3,007 hits, and compiled a .297 batting average.

Form isn't the reason. The first time anybody saw Roberto Clemente step into the batter's box for the Pittsburgh Pirates, the best guess was that Clemente would be back in Double A ball in a week. He had one foot in the bucket and held his bat at an awkward angle—he looked as though he couldn't hit an outside pitch. A lot of other ballplayers may have had a better-looking stance. Yet they never led the National League in hitting in four different years, the way Clemente did.

Not every ballplayer is born with the ability to hit a curveball. Nor is exceptional hand-eye coordination the key to heavy hitting. Big-league locker rooms are filled with players who have all the attributes, save one: discipline. Every baseball man can tell you a story about a pitcher who throws a ball faster than anyone has ever seen but who has no control on or *off* the field.

The Hall of Fame is full of people who transformed themselves into great ballplayers by working at the sport, by studying the game, and making sacrifices. They're overachievers—and winners. If you want to find them, just watch the World Series. Or simply read about New York Yankee great Lou Gehrig; Ted Williams, "the Splendid Splinter" of the Boston Red Sox; or the Dodgers' strikeout king Sandy Koufax.

A pitcher *should* be able to win a lot of ballgames with a 98-miles-per-hour fastball. But what about the pitcher who wins 20 games a year with a fastball so slow that you can catch it with your teeth? Bob Feller of the Cleveland Indians got into the Hall of Fame with a blazing fastball that glowed in the dark. National League star Grover Cleveland Alexander got there with a pitch that took considerably longer to reach the plate; but when it did arrive, the pitch was exactly where Alexander wanted it to be— and the last place the batter expected it to be.

There are probably more players with exceptional ability who didn't make it to the major leagues than there are who did. A number of great hitters, bored with fielding practice, had to be dropped from their team because their home-run production didn't make up for their lapses in the field. And then there are players like Brooks Robinson of the Baltimore Orioles, who made himself into a human vacuum cleaner at third base because he knew that working hard to become an expert fielder would win him a job in the big leagues.

A star is not something that flashes through the sky. That's a comet. Or a meteor. A star is something you can steer ships by. It stays in place and gives off a steady glow; it is fixed, permanent. A star works at being a star.

And that's how you tell a star in baseball. He shows up night after night and takes pride in how brightly he shines. He's Willie Mays running so hard his hat keeps falling off; Ty Cobb sliding to stretch a single into a double; Lou Gehrig, after being fooled in his first two at-bats, belting the next pitch off the light tower because he's taken the time to study the pitcher. Stars never take themselves for granted. That's why they're stars.

"IT AIN'T BRAGGING IF YOU CAN DO IT!"

Grantland Rice was America's favorite sports columnist when Dizzy Dean emerged as one of baseball's brightest young stars. On July 30, 1933, the Sunday newspapers across the country carried Rice's assessment of the St. Louis Cardinals pitcher: "Dean is just a kid and this is only his second season. He has the chance to be rated with the Christy Mathewsons, the Walter Johnsons, and the Grover Cleveland Alexanders. This Cardinal star has everything a great pitcher needs—more smoke than a burning oil well, a fine curve ball, good control, a cool head and plenty of heart."

As if to prove Grantland Rice knew his stuff, 21-year-old Dizzy Dean went out that afternoon and broke a 24-year-old record set first by Christy Mathewson, one of the original five players elected to the Hall of Fame. Dean, pitching in the first game of a doubleheader at Wrigley Field in Chicago, saw the first two Cubs hit safely. After one run scored, two Cardinal relievers started to warm up in the bull pen, but they were not needed. As the game got under way, the Cubs bats became silent. Inning by inning went by, and Dean's strikeout totals grew. This was not unusual. He had led the National League in strikeouts as a rookie pitcher and was currently leading it again.

By the middle of the game it appeared that Dizzy was headed for a record. Only three pitchers in baseball history had struck out as many as 16 batters in one game. Mathewson was the first; then another Hall of Famer, Rube Waddell, accomplished the feat; the last to do it, in 1909, was Nap Rucker, one of the greatest left-handers in Brooklyn Dodgers history. With two innings to go, Dean had recorded 11 strikeouts. He would have to fan the remaining six batters to set a new mark. He reared back and fired the ball, mixing in some sharp curves.

Dean struck out three straight batters in the eighth and the first two in the ninth to tie the record. The Cubs then sent up a young player, Joe Mosolf, who had a .337 career average as a pinch hitter. However, he was not eager to face Dizzy's speed. "This is a bad place to stick you in, kid," Dean's catcher, the veteran Jimmy Wilson, warned him. "I wouldn't be surprised if the first one Dizzy threw was right at your ear. He don't like pinch hitters."

"Mosolf never took the bat off his shoulder," Dizzy Dean later recalled. "Wilson'd give me the sign, and then he'd straighten up and pound his glove behind Mosolf's ear, and the guy thought he was gonna get punctured, and I just put three through there."

As soon as Mosolf became Dean's 17th strikeout victim, his teammates, who had puzzled Dean by being very quiet during the game, poured out of the dugout to carry him off the field. Dizzy finally understood why they had been so silent.

When a pitcher has a no-hitter going or has a chance to break a record, it is considered a jinx to have one's teammates talk about what is taking place.

Dizzy stood under the grandstand after the game—which he later called the greatest of his career—and signed autographs for the kids who were among the 29,500 fans at Wrigley Field. It was the largest crowd there in two years, and many had come just to see Dean pitch the opening game of the doubleheader. Then Dizzy showered and went to the press box for several innings. After that, he returned to the clubhouse and got back into his uniform—just in case, he said, the Cardinals needed him to strike out a few more Cubs.

Dizzy Dean was only 19 when he burst on the baseball scene, and he was a very talkative young man. In fact, throughout his career he was never shy about letting his teammates, opponents, and newspaper reporters know how good he was. There was nothing wrong with saying what you believed, according to the rangy right-hander from the Ozark Mountains, where it was often said, "It ain't bragging if you can do it!"

2

A STAR RECRUIT

"Them ain't lies, them is scoops" was Dizzy Dean's explanation for giving three different birth places to three different reporters. Dean said he gave out a different home town and birthday to oblige each sportswriter with an exclusive interview.

Actually, the boy who grew up to become Dizzy Dean was born on January 16, 1911, in Lucas, a sleepy, small town in southwestern Arkansas. The rootless Dean family had stopped there to spend a winter between cotton picking seasons. Every year Albert and Alma Dean and their children scratched a bare living from soil that was already starting to wear out. By the time Dizzy Dean reached the big leagues in the early 1930s, much of the topsoil on which he had grown up and first played baseball had eroded. The area came to be called "the Dust Bowl."

The Dean family: (left to right, front row) Mrs. Dizzy Dean, Albert Dean, Mrs. Paul Dean; (left to right, rear) Dizzy Dean, Elmer Dean, and Paul Dean.

Dizzy's mother named him Jay Hanna in honor of Jay Gould and Mark Hanna, two millionaire financiers of the time. When Dizzy was only three years old, he changed his name to Jerome Herman, which had been the name of a friend of his who had died. Young Dizzy told the grieving father that he would always remember his friend by taking his name as his own. Dizzy later signed his first baseball contract as J. H. Dean, and his baseball cards in the 1930s called him Jerome Herman "Dizzy" Dean. He did not use his original names again until he signed a marriage certificate. His wife called him Jay, but everyone else, from ordinary fans to United States presidents, called him Dizzy, or, as he referred to himself even when he was just a rookie, Ol' Diz.

While Dizzy was still a boy, his mother died. Left with three small sons, the hard-working Albert Dean married again, this time to a widow with a large family of her own. The two struggled to feed the whole brood and keep an orderly household.

Dizzy later claimed he developed his throwing ability by hurling rocks and clods of dirt at prairie dogs and squirrels. According to him, baseball scouts initially thought he was left-handed. "That was because they seen me killing squirrels with stones throwing left-handed. If I'd of throwed right-handed I would have squashed them." He was a lean, sinewy boy who was soon able to take his place with the men in the fields. He could pick 400 pounds of cotton. It was back-breaking work that went on day after day, beginning at dawn and continuing until the sun set.

On Sundays, the men and boys played baseball. Albert had once played professional baseball, but now he let his boys star. From the start, Dizzy was the pitcher. Sometimes his brother Paul, who

Young Dizzy Dean, while pitching for the utility company in Houston, Texas, strikes a serious pose.

was two and a half years younger than Dizzy, would play shortstop or catch. Most often, the eldest Dean boy, Elmer, whom people called "Goober," did the catching.

When Dizzy was 16, he found his way out of being an itinerant farm hand. He convinced the enlisting officer at Fort Sam Houston, Texas, that he was 18 and joined the U. S. Army's 12th Field Artillery. Pvt. Dean was paid $17.50 a month. He was given three meals a day, a place to sleep, and his first pair of brand new shoes.

It was in the army that he was first called Dizzy. He had come to the attention of Sgt. Jimmy Brought, both as a pitcher for their regiment's baseball team and as a recruit. Dean's blazing fastball made the hitters "dizzy." However, he also had an unfortunate knack for getting into trouble. The safest way for an army private to get along is not to be noticed, but that was impossible for Dean, who had an opinion about everything and talked everyone "dizzy"—hence the double-edged nickname coined by the sergeant.

Dean spent most of his enlistment either on kitchen patrol, scrubbing pots and pans in the mess hall, or "doing stables." When the artillery's caissons—chests packed with explosives—went rolling along, they were pulled by horses. The horses "outranked" the enlisted men and had to be fed and groomed, and their stalls had to be mucked out before a soldier could look after his own needs.

When Dean became a professional ball player he always seemed to make the right play. It was thought he was a natural. Actually, he had the way to play the game drilled into him on the regimental diamonds of the 12th Field Artillery ball club. Most of the service teams were well coached. In addition, the managers had complete authority. A recruit made sure to learn how the game was played when the penalty for an error might be a month of extra stable duty.

In mid-1929 after two years in the army, Dizzy, whose sinewy body had become filled out by three regular meals a day, decided he was ready to leave military life. At that time, an enlisted man could buy his way out of the army by paying $200. The other Deans were working close to where the 12th Field Artillery was training, and the family then had as much cash as it would ever scrape together.

Paul proceeded to take $200 of his share and use it to free his brother from the army.

For the rest of 1929, Dizzy worked for a public utilities company in San Antonio, Texas. His job was mainly to pitch for their Industrial League baseball team. He soon caught the eye of Don Curtis, a St. Louis Cardinals scout. After Dizzy had won 16 straight games, he signed a contract to play professional baseball.

3

"HE'S GOING TO BE A GREAT ONE"

In 1930, the St. Louis Cardinals sent Dizzy Dean to the St. Joseph, Missouri, team in the Western League. St. Louis was the first club to establish its own minor league teams and have them develop players for the parent club. The minor leagues enabled major league teams in smaller cities, such as St. Louis, to compete with wealthier squads from bigger towns. Branch Rickey, the Cardinals general manager, devised this network, which came to be called "the farm system."

On April 20, Dean won his first start, 4-3, in extra innings. Despite pitching for what proved to be a last-place club, he was an instant star. He was certainly the league's most talked about prospect, and boasted a 17-8 record when he was promoted to the Cardinals' Texas League team, the Houston Buffaloes.

The 1930 Texas League season ended on Labor Day, with Dizzy winning his eighth game in his four

At Ray Doan's Baseball School in Hot Springs, Arkansas, Dizzy demonstrates the fine points of pitching.

19

weeks with Houston. Then the St. Louis Cardinals, who were in a hot pennant race that had a month to go, called him up. Having already won 25 games—8 for Houston and 17 for St. Joseph—he expected to nail down the pennant for the Cardinals.

Despite Dean's outstanding record in 1930, Gabby Street, the St. Louis manager, kept his prize rookie on the bench. His team was fighting for the pennant, and he had a string of veteran pitchers who were winning. The Cardinals finally edged out the Chicago Cubs in St. Louis on the next to last day of the season. Only then did the manager let Dizzy pitch. As the lean, tall right-hander warmed up, the mayor of St. Louis, who had come to Sportsman's Park to salute the new league

Dizzy struck out this trio of future Hall of Famers on nine pitches. (Left to right) Jimmie Foxx, Mickey Cochrane, and Al Simmons combined to hit 960 major-league home runs.

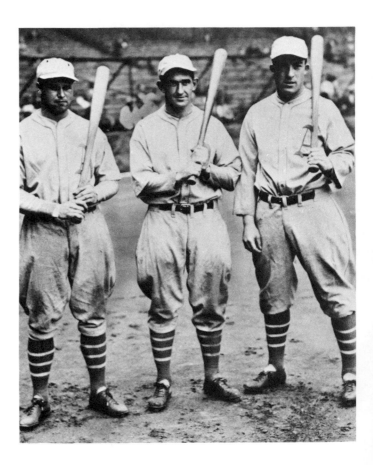

champions, asked Manager Street, "Is this fellow Dean going to be as good as they say?"

"I think he's going to be a great one, Mr. Mayor," Gabby assured him. Then Street made one of the most prophetic observations in baseball history. "But I'm afraid we'll never know from one minute to the next what he's going to do or say."

On September 28, 1930, Dizzy Dean made his spectacular debut. He allowed only three singles and won his first major-league game, beating the Pittsburgh Pirates, 3–1. Because he joined St. Louis so late in the season, he was not eligible to play in the World Series, which the Cardinals lost to the Philadelphia Athletics.

After the 1930 season, Dean went back to St. Joseph and spent the winter at the home of Oliver French, the business manager of the Cardinals' farm club there. French had promised Branch Rickey he would keep Dean in shape and out of trouble, and he was true to his word. When Dizzy reported to spring training in Bradenton, Florida, to get ready for the Cardinals' 1931 season he was full of confidence and as talkative as ever.

Once again Manager Street kept Dean on the bench. He was not allowed to pitch until the world champion Philadelphia Athletics came to town to play an exhibition game. Street waited until the late innings, when he knew the first three batters would be Mickey Cochrane, Al Simmons, and Jimmie Foxx, before inserting Dean into the lineup. Everyone expected these three batters, who are now members of the Baseball Hall of Fame, to silence Dizzy. Instead, they were easy victims as Dean struck them out on nine straight pitches.

Despite the ability Dizzy showed, the Cardinal management decided to give their young pitcher the sobering experience of another year in the minor leagues. It might not make him a better pitcher, but it might make him a lot easier to put up with. When spring training ended, the Cardinals headed north without Dizzy Dean. "That's the only time a team ever lost 30 games in one day," observed Jim Lindsey, a Cardinal pitcher.

The Cardinals won the pennant again in 1931. Considering that the staff, which won 101 games, lacked a 20-game winner, the addition of Dean could have made the team among the greatest of all time. Dizzy read the daily box scores in the Houston newspapers as the Cardinals breezed to the pennant and demolished the Athletics in the World Series. It should have been a humbling experience for the confident Dizzy Dean, but it was not, and although he was pitching against minor-league competition, his feats were truly remarkable. Dizzy led the Texas League with 26 wins and 303 strikeouts (18 of them in one game) and an earned run average of 1.57. He was also named the league's Most Valuable Player. However, it was not his baseball experiences that shaped the rest of his life, it was his meeting Patricia Nash, who came from Bond, Mississippi. She was a department store sales clerk in Houston when Dizzy spun her through a whirlwind courtship. He failed to talk her into getting married at home plate, but he did persuade her to become Mrs. Dean. It was the best thing that could have happened to the exuberant farm boy. The new bride was the perfect mate for the carefree young pitcher. She balanced her husband's impulsive spending sprees with her own thrifty nature and managed to save $1,200 of the $3,000 salary he was paid the first year they were married. Pat Dean became the guiding hand the strong-armed pitcher needed.

*Before boarding an air-
plane, Dizzy and Pat Dean,
along with Paul Dean, talk
to sports writers. Airplane
travel for sports teams was
rare in the 1930s, but
baseball teams sometimes
had their pitchers fly to a
city ahead of the team. The
pitchers could then rest up
for their next pitching
assignment.*

"Somebody in the family has to have practical
sense," she said. "Dizzy's got it in a ball game and
it's up to me to have it for both of us off the field.
Dizzy's sitting on top of the world now. But I've
heard cheers change to jeers in one breath. Sport
fans are the most fickle persons in the world. The
higher you go the harder you fall, and when the
crowds start booing my Dizzy, I want him to have
the money to retire gracefully. It won't be a bench
in the park for him, if I can help it."

Dizzy enjoyed his first full major-league season
in 1932, a season that had all the elements that
would keep his name in the headlines throughout
his career. A bout with the flu delayed the beginning of his season until late April. In his second
start, he pitched a 9–0 shutout to beat Cincinnati.
In his third start, he hit two doubles while beating
New York, 6–5. Overall, he won 18 games for a
seventh-place team. Dizzy's season was one of the
few things that fans of the defending world

Dean and his teammate, Pepper Martin. It was Martin's aggressive spirit and head-first slides that inspired the Cardinals' nickname "the Gashouse Gang."

champions could cheer about as the rookie led the league in strikeouts and innings pitched.

Dizzy Dean's rookie season established him as the successor to Babe Ruth as America's favorite player. The talkative young pitcher from rural America received publicity for more than just his baseball skills. When the Cardinals booked a rodeo as a pre-game feature to help draw people to the closing game of the schedule, Dizzy joined in. He missed lassoing a calf from the back of his horse, so he jumped down and wrestled the calf to the ground as the crowd cheered.

In 1933, Dean had his first 20-game winning season, although the Cardinals again finished in the second division.

Before the season was over, Gabby Street, who had won pennants in 1930 and 1931, was let go as manager, and the fiery second baseman Frank Frisch was put in charge. "The Dutchman," as

Dean called the college graduate most fans knew as "The Fordham Flash," was to have numerous battles with his star pitcher. Dean was never comfortable with authority figures, whether they were army sergeants, managers, or team owners.

Before the month of July was over, Dizzy had made the headlines with his record-breaking 17-strikeout game in Chicago. He was given a medal for the achievement and at Christmas he sent out personal cards showing the medal and a picture of him pitching in the 17-strikeout game.

In late December, the Deans set up house in Bradenton, Florida, where the Cardinals did their spring training. When the other Cardinals got together in March, he was in fine shape. The team that Frank Frisch, in his first full season as manager, would lead had changed in key positions from the team that finished the previous season in the second division. Joe "Ducky" Medwick, who had a fine rookie season in 1933, would be even better with experience. Ripper Collins, a switch-hitting slugger, would provide the punch. Pepper Martin, "the Wild Horse of the Osage," had moved from the outfield to third base. Frank Frisch was still considered one of the best second basemen in the National League and would be paired with the best-fielding shortstop in baseball, Leo "the Lip" Durocher, who had come to the Cardinals from the Giants during the previous season. Jack Rothrock, a former American League utility player who had played all nine positions in a 1928 game for the Boston Red Sox, would play every inning in 1934. And there were two new catchers, veteran Spud Davis and a rookie, Bill DeLancey. Both would hit over .300 and divide the catching. Dizzy Dean was the ace of the staff. And there was a new pitcher on the team: Paul Dean, Dizzy's kid brother.

4

"ME 'N' PAUL"

In 1934, there was no night baseball. There was no public address system; a man shouted the lineups to the crowd through a megaphone. There had been radio broadcasts since 1926, but they were ended in 1934 because the owners believed people would stay at home during those bleak Depression days and listen to the games rather than pay to see the team.

Not seeing much new about the team, many sportswriters thought that the most exciting change to the 1934 Cardinals was that there were now two Dean brothers. At first the sportswriters tried to turn Paul, almost three years younger than the colorful Dizzy, into a duplicate by nicknaming him Daffy. It did not work. Paul was the opposite in personality to his talkative brother. However, they were very much alike as pitchers.

Paul was an inch shorter than the 6'3" Dizzy

Quiet Paul Dean was happy to let Dizzy do most of the talking for the two brothers, and Dizzy was glad to oblige. "Anybody who's ever had the privilege of seein' me play ball knows that I am the greatest pitcher in the world," Dizzy once declared.

and a few pounds lighter. Both threw with a three-quarters motion and had a blazing fastball. Paul was not someone who was looking to make it in the big leagues off his big brother's reputation. Paul had been 22–7 and had led the American Association in strikeouts in his third season in the minor leagues.

The Dean brothers were inseparable. Naturally, Dizzy did all the talking, with the quiet younger brother nodding his agreement. The big change was that the boasts now began "Me 'n' Paul." Dizzy insisted his kid brother was the better pitcher. There was no jealousy between the two young men. Each was genuinely excited by the success of the other.

Paul lived with Dizzy and Pat when the team was in St. Louis and roomed with a fellow rookie, catcher Bill DeLancey, when the team was on the road because the Cardinals encouraged Pat Dean to travel with her husband on road trips, thinking she would be a good influence on him.

At the Cardinals' spring training camp in Bradenton, Dizzy not only assured everyone that he and Paul would win 45 to 50 games, he campaigned for a salary increase for both of them. Dizzy had been upset to learn that veteran pitcher Bill Hallahan, who had formerly been the team's star, was paid more than the combined salaries of the Dean brothers. It was a sore point with the Deans all spring and into the season that Paul drew only $3,000 and Diz $7,500. They complained of sore arms and kept threatening to quit and pitch for independent teams.

Dizzy won the opening-day game, then faltered during the early season. Paul, who pitched only six innings in spring training, was slow to work his way into the starting rotation. The team began slowly as well and stayed in the second division until the middle of May. Then the Deans began to win, particularly against the New York Giants, the pre-season favorites to repeat as champions. Paul, who like Dizzy would beat the Giants six times during the season, won his first eight decisions. He did not lose a game from mid-May until June 20. Dizzy won ten straight during June and July, but the Deans were the team's only consistent winners.

The 1934 pennant race settled into a three-team chase with the Cubs and Giants ahead of the third-place Cards when baseball stopped for its new mid-season event, the All-Star Game. This had been played for the first time in 1933. Dizzy, a rookie that year, had not been on the team.

In the 1934 game, Dizzy's arch rival, Carl Hubbell of the Giants, was the starting National League pitcher and performed the legendary feat of striking out five future Hall of Famers in a row:

At spring training in 1934, Dizzy hands his brother Paul a Cardinals contract to sign. Paul was the top pitcher with the Columbus, Ohio, Cubs in 1933.

Babe Ruth, Lou Gehrig, Jimmie Foxx, Al Simmons, and Joe Cronin. Dizzy pitched three innings, giving up one run and striking out four. However, the American League won, 9–7.

Dizzy hated to lose, and on August 12 he and Paul were the losing pitchers in a doubleheader with the Cubs. The next day, the Cardinals were due in Detroit for an exhibition game with the Tigers. But the Deans remained behind in St. Louis. Even though they would not have pitched, the fans expected the Deans to appear. Manager Frank Frisch suspended the brothers and fined Dizzy $100 and Paul $50. The outraged Dizzy tore up his white home uniform and when the photographers asked him to do it again, he ripped his grey road uniform apart.

Dizzy then went to Chicago to appeal to the baseball commissioner, Judge Landis, to have the fines dropped and to be reinstated with his brother. Landis ordered a hearing to be held several days

Dean signs autographs for his young fans.

later in St. Louis. There he shocked Dizzy by saying the star pitchers were at fault. Paul gave in first, and Dizzy returned to action on August 25, pitching the Cardinals into second place by beating the Giants, 6–0.

Fans, siding with the Deans against management, mailed Dizzy more than $1,000 to cover the fines and lost salary due to the suspension. However, Dizzy sent all the money back with notes of thanks and promises of better behavior. While Dizzy was suspended, his unsympathetic teammates had won seven of eight games. On Labor Day, September 3, the Deans again lost a doubleheader, this time to Pittsburgh. Although the losses dropped the team seven games behind the Giants, the Dean brothers continued to pitch valiantly.

On September 16, at the Polo Grounds, the best pitchers on both teams faced each other in a doubleheader. Dizzy beat the Giants' Hal Schumacher, who would win 23 games in 1934,

Dizzy and Paul Dean look over the camera work of Warner Brothers producer Sam Sax (holding camera) while the St. Louis Cardinal treasurer, Bill DeWitt, who handled the Deans' non-baseball business interests, peers over Sax's shoulder. The Deans were the stars of a 1935 Warner Brothers movie called "Dizzy and Daffy," billed as a "light-hearted comedy."

and Paul defeated Carl Hubbell, whose season total would be 21. This left the Cardinals 3½ games behind with the season winding down.

With only two weeks left in the season, the Cardinals came to Brooklyn's Ebbets Field for a doubleheader. The Dean brothers shut out the Dodgers in both games. Dizzy held Brooklyn hitless until two were out in the eighth, then Paul followed with a no-hit game. Afterward, Dizzy boasted, "The only thing that makes me mad is that Paul didn't tell me he was gonna throw a no-hitter. If I'd a known that, I would have throwed one too."

The Cardinals surge continued, and the Giants kept stumbling until the pennant race reached the

The Dean brothers celebrate after Paul's no-hitter, a 3–0 win against the Dodgers in the second game of a doubleheader on September 21. Dizzy won the first game, 13–0, and had a no-hitter of his own until the eighth inning.

final weekend of the season. Dizzy, who won five of the Cardinals last 16 games, pitched the team into a tie with the Giants on Friday. He beat the Reds, 4–0.

Before the 1934 season began, the Giants' manager, Bill Terry, had scoffed at the lowly Dodgers. "Brooklyn? Are they still in the league?" he had asked sarcastically. The loyal Dodger fans, their team deep in the second division, would consider the season a success if it kept its crosstown rivals, the Giants, from taking the pennant. Fate decreed that the season would end with the Dodgers invading the Polo Grounds for the final two games.

On Saturday, the vengeful Dodgers and thousands of their fans arrived at the Polo Grounds. While Paul Dean was winning in St. Louis, defeating Cincinnati, 6–1, the Brooklyn ace, Van Lingle Mungo, was beating the Giants, 5–1. The Cardinals had taken first place with one game left for each team to play.

On the final Sunday of the season, the Giants could regain a tie only if they won and the Cardinals lost. Once again, the Dodgers humbled the Giants while Dizzy was making sure of the pennant with his 30th win of the season. No National League pitcher since has won as many.

5

THE DEAN SERIES

There was jubilation in St. Louis and despair in New York when the 1934 regular season ended. Before the cheering had stopped for the happy Cardinals, Dizzy Dean, with hardly time to catch his breath, was predicting what would happen when St. Louis met the well-rested and favored Detroit Tigers. He assured everyone of a Cardinal victory even if "me 'n' Paul" had to win all four games. Then, with only two days rest, he proceeded to make good on his promise.

The 1934 World Series opened in Detroit. The Cardinals had traveled by train, arriving there a day early so they could hold a practice. But Dizzy, who arrived at the ballpark while the Tigers were still taking batting practice, did not bother to put on his uniform. He simply took off his suit coat and rolled up his shirt sleeves. "Here," he told the astonished Detroit manager, Mickey Cochrane, "let a feller who knows how show you the way to

Dizzy Dean, School Boy Rowe, and Paul Dean, the pitching aces for the two 1934 World Series rivals. The Dean brothers each won two games, while Rowe managed just one win, a magnificent 12-inning effort in game 2. During one stretch, the Detroit star retired 22 Cardinals in a row.

*In game 4 of the 1934
World Series, Dean pinch
ran for the Cardinals slow-
moving catcher, Virgil Davis.
On a double-play grounder,
Dean came into second
base standing up, and Billy
Rogell's relay throw hit him
in the back of the head.
Dean was taken off the field
on a stretcher, but X rays
indicated no serious
damage.*

hit." He took the bat from Cochrane, stepped into the batter's box, and drove a pitch into the left-field stands. Dizzy then sat on the Tigers bench and joked with the enemy. In the Cardinal clubhouse, he posed with a rubber tiger. He twisted it into strange shapes and told the photographers he'd do the same to Detroit the next day.

Dizzy was not quite as good as his word, but he did not have to be. The Tigers, trying too hard to prove Dean wrong, suffered World Series jitters, making five errors. Dean struggled, going three and two on most batters, giving up eight hits and three runs. However, the Cardinals, led by Joe Medwick's four hits, a home run among them, scored eight runs to give Dizzy an easy 8–3 win.

The Tigers' ace, Schoolboy Rowe, who had won 16 straight during the season and 24 in all, outlasted Bill Hallahan in the second game. The Tigers won, 3–2, in 12 innings. There was no pause, even though the teams had to travel, and the World Series resumed the following day in St.

Louis, with Paul Dean on the mound. He pitched an eight-hitter, giving up a lone run in the ninth inning while coasting to a 4–1 victory.

The next day the Tigers again evened the Series. Underhand-style pitcher Eldon Auker went all the way for a 10–4 win. Dizzy got into the game and out of it right away. In the fourth inning, when the Cardinals were rallying to tie the score at 4–4, Dizzy dashed onto the field to be a pinch-runner. When the batter hit a routine double play ball, Dizzy went into second base standing up. The throw to first base by the Tiger shortstop, Billy Rogell, bounced off Dean's head. He had broken up the double play, but he also had to be carried off the field on a stretcher. The next day's newspapers ran a headline: *X rays of Dean's Head Show Nothing.*

Instead of remaining in the hospital, Dizzy took the mound for the fifth game. Tommy Bridges, a curveballer who had won 22 games for the Tigers, took the mound with just one day's rest. He outpitched Dizzy 3–1, as Gehringer homered against Dean in the seventh inning. Now the teams traveled back to Detroit with the Tigers just one victory away from the championship.

Paul Dean kept the Cardinals' hopes alive. With the game tied at three runs apiece, Paul came to bat in the seventh inning against Schoolboy Rowe and drove in what proved to be the winning run in a 4–3 victory. This set the dramatic scene for his brother's greatest win.

Many people doubted that Dizzy would start the final game with only a day's rest. Manager Frank Frisch had hinted he would use a pitcher who was not as tired as his ace. But Dizzy Dean had no doubt as to who would be on the mound when the final game began.

This button is from a set of 25 baseball-player buttons issued in the mid-1930s by "Button Gum."

The Tigers and their fans wanted Dizzy to pitch, too. They were seething mad and wanted to humble the boastful Dean. Instead, Dizzy began to embarrass the Tigers. A better-than-average batter and base runner, he dropped a single in front of leftfielder Goose Goslin with the game scoreless in the third inning. When the veteran outfielder loafed after the ball, Dean lit out for second base. Goslin's throw was on line, but Dizzy avoided the tag.

Pepper Martin, the next batter, hit a ground ball to the right of first baseman Hank Greenberg. If Dizzy had stopped at first, as everyone had expected him to, the Tigers probably would have turned an easy double play. Instead, Greenberg checked Dean at second but threw too late to first to get the speedy Martin. Meanwhile, Dean was sliding safely into third. Looking to set up a double play, the Tigers loaded the bases by walking the next batter, Jack Rothrock.

The Cardinals playing manager, Frank Frisch, himself a future Hall of Fame member, was next to step to the plate. He ripped a double down the right-field foul line to clear the bases. Those three runs would have been enough the way Dizzy Dean was pitching, but before the inning ended, the Cardinals had a seven-run lead. Dizzy tied a record for pitchers in the World Series by getting a second hit in the same inning.

Dean never let up on the Tigers. The Cardinals, a rough and ready lot known as the Gashouse Gang, shouted insults from the bench. When the game reached the sixth inning, there was little doubt who would win. Joe Medwick, running out a triple, slid hard into Marv Owen at third. Medwick's hard slide added injury to insult in the eyes of the Tiger fans, and when he returned to the outfield

they pelted him with a barrage of fruit and vegetables. Three times Medwick went to take his position, and three times he was driven back.

Finally, baseball commissioner Kenesaw Mountain Landis, watching from his field box, summoned the two managers, Frisch and Cochrane, as well as Medwick and Owen. With the score 9–0, Landis decided to remove Medwick from the game rather than forfeit the contest to St. Louis.

Dizzy strutted through the final innings, in particular taunting the Tigers' cleanup hitter, Hank Greenberg, who had driven in 139 runs during the regular season. Dean had already struck him out twice when the slugger came to bat in the ninth inning. Dean looked over at the Detroit manager, the hot-tempered Mickey Cochrane, and suggested that he send up a pinch-hitter. Dean's

Manager Frankie Frisch and Dean celebrate after the 1934 Series victory. Frisch said of Dean: "Without Dizzy we'd never even be in the pennant race. There has never, ever been a pitching character like Dizzy Dean in the history of the game."

own manager, Frank Frisch, dashed in from second base. Despite an 11–0 lead, Frisch was in no mood for further joking from Dizzy. He threatened to take him out of the game.

Dizzy waved Greenberg into the batter's box, and once again the Tiger home run king fanned. The game was over a moment later and the Cardinals were the 1934 World Champions. Dizzy Dean had put his personal stamp on the climactic game and finished the greatest season he would ever have.

The Deans, badly underpaid by the Cardinals, made up for it by what they earned after the season ended. The winning share of the World Series money was over $5,000 for each player. "Barnstorming games," as off-season exhibition games were called, netted Dizzy another $5,700. He endorsed breakfast cereals, a harmonica, hats, school writing tablets, a table baseball game, wrist watches, sweatshirts, pants, and whatever else someone would pay him to approve. He appeared on network radio as a guest with the entertainers

Al Jolson and Kate Smith. The brothers even appeared on the vaudeville stage. It all added up to more than $40,000.

Dizzy was also cited as the National League's Most Valuable Player. At that time, there was no Cy Young Award for the best pitcher in the league, and to become MVP meant being picked over all the other players in the league, not just the pitchers.

Dizzy Dean had won 30 games and saved seven others. He had led the National League in wins, winning percentage, complete games, shutouts, and, of course, his specialty, strikeouts. Claiming "me 'n' Paul will win forty-five between us," he had underestimated their final tally. However, his prediction that they would win all four World Series games had been right on the mark.

6

POPPIN' OFF

Dizzy Dean rode a wave of popularity into 1935. Babe Ruth's career with the New York Yankees had ended, but he tried to hang on by moving to the National League with the Boston Braves. The first time baseball's new idol, Dizzy Dean, met the fading Ruth, he struck him out, and it was the young pitcher who hit a home run. When the Babe called it quits, Dizzy was happy to claim the spotlight.

Once again he boasted, "Me 'n' Paul will win at least forty-five games between us." And he would be right again. Only this season his 28 wins and Paul's second 19-victory season would not be enough to win a pennant. Instead, the Chicago Cubs would win 19 straight games in the closing weeks of the season for the National League title.

What was even worse, the fun-loving Cardinal pitcher found out that the fans would not put up with his sometimes selfish behavior. In an early season game with Pittsburgh, Dizzy thought the umpire was making bad calls and began lobbing the ball to the plate. The delighted Pirate batters rattled base hits off the fences. Between innings,

Dizzy and Paul flank the 40-year-old Babe Ruth, starting his 1935 season as a Boston Brave. Ruth slugged 3 home runs in a May 25th game, but hitting just .181, he announced his retirement on June 2nd.

"The Gashouse Gang," a name given to the Cardinals of the early 1930s by Frank Graham of the New York Sun: (left to right) Dean, Leo Durocher, Ernie Orsatti, Bill DeLancey, Jack Rothrock, Joe Medwick, Frank Frisch, Rip Collins, Pepper Martin.

Dean argued with his teammates, who did not like what he was doing. Finally, manager Frisch took him out of the game.

Just as his wife had predicted, the public turned on their hero, and Dizzy's popularity dropped. Stores could not sell the merchandise that had his name on it. He was still winning at the ball park, but he was losing favor with the fans. The year before, he got into trouble by refusing to go with the team to play an exhibition game. This time, when a game was scheduled in St. Paul, Minnesota, he and Paul went, but they sulked in the dugout. The talkative Dizzy would not even come out to take a bow and say a few words on the public address system.

To his credit, Dean realized he had "popped off" once too often and wrote a letter to George Edmond, sports editor of the St. Paul *Dispatch*: "I want to apologize to the fans of St. Paul. I am just a young

fellow, and I hope the fans all over the country will be patient with me as I know I'm not perfect and do make a few mistakes once in a while."

Dizzy's sudden humility got him back in the good graces of the public, and he was named to the 1935 All-Star team. Nevertheless, manager Frank Frisch, in charge of the National League team, started another Cardinal pitcher, Bill Walker, and by the time Dizzy took his turn in the final inning, the game was lost.

Dizzy and the Gashouse Gang were as full of fun as ever as the 1935 season rolled along. Their stunts got the team thrown out of three hotels in Philadelphia alone. The ringleaders were usually Dizzy and Pepper Martin. One time, they and a couple of teammates put on painter's overalls and dropped in on a banquet room where a local Boy Scout dinner was going on. Carrying ladders and paint brushes, they began moving people away

from the main table and noisily rearranging the furniture. The main speaker was stunned. "Well, " Dizzy said, "If you're not going to make a speech, I will. Sit down, I'll take care of this." The boys recognized Dizzy Dean and cheered when he took over the meeting.

The next season was the end of "Me 'n' Paul." Although Dizzy continued to be a workhorse, leading the league in 1936 with 315 innings pitched, winning 24 games and saving 11 others, Paul developed a sore arm and won only 5 games. His career was over. He would make comeback attempts but without success. The Cardinals finished behind the Giants in a tie for second place with the Cubs.

The 1937 season proved to be the beginning of the end for Dizzy, too. His battles on and off the field were spectacular. He even used spring training to get ready for the regular season scraps. In Tampa, Florida, he objected to remarks made by a New York columnist, Jack Milery, and fists flew when they met in a hotel lobby. Teammates and other writers joined in.

Dizzy started the season with five straight wins, but everyone's attention was on his great rival, Carl Hubbell. The New York Giant ace had finished 1936 with 16 straight wins and was also unbeaten in 1937 when "Hub" and "Diz" met on May 21 in St. Louis. It was the eighth time they had gone head-to-head. Hubbell evened their series to extend his win streak. Dean, however, got the headlines. When umpire George Barr called a third balk against him, Dizzy began throwing at the Giants batters. Finally, one of them, Jimmy Ripple, rushed out to the mound, and Dizzy disappeared under a pile of New York players. The Cardinals came to the rescue, peeling Giants off the pile and squaring off in one-on-one fights. The free-for-all went on for 20 minutes, with just about everyone swinging away. The only one who sat out the battle was Carl Hubbell, who watched from the dugout. When the brawl was over, he quietly resumed pitching and added to his streak. It would end a week later, giving him a record of 24 consecutive victories.

The day after the brawl, Dizzy Dean announced he would pass up the All-Star Game and two days later made a farce of a game by taking 11 minutes to make three pitches. He was still upset about the balks that had been called on him. "You can't commit a balk if you don't pitch," he said in defense of his delaying the game.

Dizzy kept the argument going when he spoke at a local father and son banquet. He was alleged

Yankee slugger Lou Gehrig chats with Dizzy before the start of the 1937 All Star game. Gehrig, who came into the game hitting .349, hit a 3 and 2 pitch from Dean for a two-run first-inning homer.

to have called Ford Frick, the National League president, and umpire George Barr "the two biggest crooks in baseball." Frick demanded that the pitcher apologize and prepared a letter for him to sign. Dean would not do it. Finally, the league president backed down.

The following week, Dizzy beat his old rival, Carl Hubbell, in the last game in which the two would meet.

Dean eventually agreed to pitch in the All-Star Game, but it would have been far better if he had stayed away. He started the game and was one out from finishing three scoreless innings when he shook off the catcher's signal for a curve and tried to "fog one," as he described his fast ball, past Lou Gehrig. The Yankee slugger drove the pitch over the right field wall for a two-run homer. But the real damage was done by Earl Averill, the next batter. He smashed a line drive back at the pitcher and it hit Dizzy on the foot. Dean limped off the field. When his foot was X-rayed, it was learned that the big toe on his left foot was fractured. He was told to rest until the injury had healed. Always a game competitor, Dizzy insisted on pitching before the toe was back to normal. Unable to put full pressure on his injured toe, he used an unnatural motion and developed a sore arm. When he tried to pitch, he could not throw without agonizing pain.

Dizzy Dean won only one more game in 1937 after the All-Star Game. On August 22, he staggered to a complete game victory, 9–7, over the Pittsburgh Pirates in what proved to be his last win as a Cardinal.

That winter, the St. Louis Cardinals general manager, Branch Rickey, was delighted when William Wrigley, the Chicago Cubs owner, insisted upon buying the damaged Dean. Rickey warned

Wrigley that Diz had a sore arm, but the Cubs paid $185,000 to bring Dizzy Dean to Chicago.

As it turned out, it was a smart investment. True, Dizzy could only pitch once in a great while and had to use his head, not his arm, to get the batters out. But his control was better than ever, and he won seven games while losing only one. It was not like previous Dizzy Dean seasons, but those seven victories brought fans out to the park and helped the Cubs win the 1938 pennant.

The New York Yankees had won their third straight American League pennant, and with their

In the 1938 pennant race, Dean was called on by player-manager Hartnett to stop the first-place Pirates on September 27. "I never had nothin'," Dean confessed, "I couldn't break a pane of glass and I knew it. But I pitched." Dean shut out Pittsburgh for 8 innings and the Cubs won, 2-1, to set up a dramatic Cubs win the following day.

Cubs catcher Gabby Hartnett, who took over as manager in July 1938 and drove the Cubs to a pennant, scores the run that put the Cubs in first place to stay. Hartnett's dramatic September 28th home run, called "the homer in the gloamin'" because it was hit in the early evening semi-darkness, broke a ninth inning 5-5 tie with the Pirates.

lineup of sluggers were heavy favorites to win the World Series. They won the opening game, 3–1, with Red Ruffing beating the Cubs' best pitcher, Big Bill Lee. The Cubs next asked Dizzy Dean to try and stop the mighty Yankees. With nothing left but his reputation and heart, he flirted with fate for seven innings. The Yankees got two fluke runs in the second inning when two Cub infielders bumped into each other and let an easy ground ball score two baserunners. The Cubs came back, though, and Dizzy nursed a 3–2 lead going into the eighth inning. After an opening single, Dizzy got the first two Yankees on force outs. Just four outs to go and Dean would be a hero.

With Frank Crosetti, the third batter up, Dizzy sneaked what looked like a third strike past him. But the umpire called it a ball. The usually weak-hitting shortstop then pulled the next pitch over the left field wall at Wrigley Field for a two-run homer.

Dizzy shouted after Crosetti as he circled the bases, "If I had my old fast ball, you wouldn't have seen the ball." Crosetti agreed. "Darned if I don't think you're right, Diz," he said as he touched home plate. When Joe DiMaggio also homered with a runner on in the ninth, catcher-manager Gabby Hartnett called for time and waved reliever Larry French in from the bullpen. A tired Dizzy Dean trudged off the field to louder cheers than the courageous pitcher had ever heard when he was "foggin' 'em in" in his prime.

The Cubs were down two games to none as the two teams moved to New York, where the Yankees wrapped up the Series in four straight.

Dean's last honor during his playing career came after the 1938 season. The baseball writers voted him "the most courageous athlete of the year."

Dizzy Dean did not surrender to fate willingly. He kept trying to pitch. He would rest a few days, or a week, between pitching appearances, but the blazing speed was gone. He won nine games and lost seven during the next two seasons. He went back to the Texas League where, in 1931, he had been the MVP. But his fastball was gone, and he had to retire.

Dizzy then became a coach for the Chicago Cubs. He represented the team when the National Baseball Hall of Fame and Museum was dedicated on June 12, 1939, in Cooperstown, New York. But that was not to be the last time America would hear from Dizzy Dean. The talkative pitcher took up a new career, a natural for Dizzy Dean. He became a radio broadcaster for the home games of the St. Louis teams, the Cardinals and Browns. He was soon a star in another field.

Dizzy Dean with his announcing partner, Pee Wee Reese, former Dodger shortstop. Pee Wee's style was straightforward, while Dizzy constantly mispronounced names: "Slooter" for Slaughter, "Scarn" for Skowron, and "Stingle" for Stengel.

Just by being himself, ungrammatical and uninhibited, the broadcasts by Dizzy Dean were often more entertaining than the games he was describing. Many school teachers complained that he misused the English language. They wanted him to stop saying, "He slud into third" and "The runners have returned to their respectable bases." Dizzy entertained the radio fans, however, and he was smart enough to know that if he tried to talk like other radio announcers, the sponsors would hire someone to replace him.

Dizzy described ball games in a colorful way that his listeners could understand. Unlike many announcers of the day, he was not afraid to say what he thought was wrong, and why. His frankness got him into trouble sometimes, and once it even got him back into a big-league uniform. He had been critical of the St. Louis Browns' pitching staff, and when he said on the air that he could pitch better himself, owner Bill DeWitt gave him a chance. The last place Browns closed out the 1947 season with Dizzy Dean on the mound.

The overweight veteran huffed and bluffed his way through four scoreless innings against the White Sox. Then he lined a hit into left field and, just as he had in the 1934 World Series, he stretched it into a double, sliding into second base. When he got up limping, his wife, Pat, had seen enough. "Get him out of there before he kills himself," she shouted to manager Muddy Ruel. Mercifully, he did. Dean closed his American League career with an earned run average of 0.00 and a batting average of 1.000.

Dizzy Dean took his country boy ways to New York City and made converts of Yankee fans in 1950, doing radio broadcasts with Mel Allen. He later teamed with ex-big leaguer Buddy Blatner on radio and pioneered early television broadcasts of baseball. For 10 years, he was the announcer for the CBS-TV "Game of the Week" with Pee Wee Reese, the former Dodgers captain. A whole new public learned to love the outgoing Dizzy Dean. He wore a white western-style hat, acted the role of "a good ol' boy," and, when there was a lull in the action, he sang his favorite country song, "The Wabash Cannonball." Everyone was his "podnuh" and flocked to the theaters to see his film biography, "The Pride of St. Louis," when the movie came out in 1952.

In 1953, baseball paid Dizzy Dean its highest honor. He was elected to the Baseball Hall of Fame, topping the voting by America's baseball writers. Joe DiMaggio, on the ballot for the first time, came in eighth.

An aging Dizzy Dean managed to hold the Chicago White Sox to just three hits while shutting them out for four innings on September 27, 1947.

Actor Dan Dailey, wearing Dean's number, 17, starred as Dizzy in the 1952 film biography The Pride of St. Louis. *Actress Joanne Dru played Pat Dean, while Paul Dean was played by Richard Crenna.*

At the induction ceremony, Dizzy Dean thanked everyone for honoring him. Then he had a word for the hundreds of youngsters in the audience. "Look," he said, serious for once. "My mother passed away when I was three years old. That left my father and two brothers down there in the cotton fields of Arkansas. I want you boys to realize what a great opportunity you have in baseball. I hope all of you make this Hall of Fame. You have to practice and work hard. Give everything you have."

As with most of his life, the broadcasting career of Dizzy Dean was marked with conflicts with authority. Just as he had battled baseball owners and officials, he would not bend to sponsors and networks. He refused to do broadcasts sponsored by cigarette advertisers. He had quit smoking and did not want to encourage youngsters to start.

Finally, the networks decided Dizzy was too

old-fashioned. They wanted younger faces and former players whom the younger members of the audience had seen play. Dizzy retired from broadcasting network games, and he and Pat Dean settled in her home town of Bond, Mississippi. Dean owned a garage and filling station in Wiggens, three miles away. Still, he was in demand as a speaker and traveled widely. For relaxation, he played golf and won side bets by combining his natural athletic skill with an ability to unsettle his opponents with his non-stop talking. One time on a golf course, President Dwight D. Eisenhower asked Dean, who let himself balloon to almost 300 pounds in his last years, "Dizzy, for a man who can play golf so well, how can you permit yourself to get so overweight?"

"Mr. President," Dizzy replied, "I was on a diet for twenty-five years. Now that I'm makin' some money, I'm makin' sure I eat good to make up for the lean years."

Dean was in Reno, Nevada, amusing himself at the blackjack tables on July 15 when he had a heart attack and was rushed to the hospital. The 63-year-old former pitcher tried to talk the nurses into letting him go home, but his condition was much worse than he thought. Two days later, on July 17, 1974, with his wife and brother Paul at his bedside, Dizzy Dean died. A big funeral was held at the Baptist church in Wiggens, and Jay Hanna Dean was buried in the cemetery at Bond, Mississippi.

Dizzy Dean's words lived on, however. He had never been modest about his ball-playing ability, even in his later years, when someone would ask, "Diz, were you the greatest pitcher of them all?" He would announce, "Well, podnah, if I wasn't then I sure was amongst 'em."

CHRONOLOGY

Jan. 16, 1911	Born Jay Hanna Dean in Lucas, Arkansas
1928-29	Enlists in the U.S. Army. Nicknamed "Dizzy"
Apr. 20, 1930	Makes debut in organized baseball with St. Louis Cardinal farm team in St. Joseph, Missouri
Aug. 5, 1930	Promoted to Houston in the Texas League
Sept. 28, 1930	Wins first major league start, 3–1
June 10, 1931	Marries Patricia Nash
1931	Pitches Houston to pennant and is named MVP
1932	With St. Louis Cards, leads NL in strikeouts
July 30, 1933	Strikes out 17 Cubs
1933	Leads NL in strikeouts
1934	Wins 30 games, again leads NL in strikeouts, named National League Most Valuable Player
Oct. 9, 1934	Wins final game of World Series, beating Detroit, 11–0
1935	Leads NL in strikeouts and wins with 28
July 7, 1937	Toe is fractured while pitching in All-Star Game. Arm injury follows
Apr. 16, 1938	Traded to Chicago Cubs
Oct. 6, 1938	Loses to Yankees in game 2 of the World Series
June 3, 1940	Returns to Texas League with Tulsa
July 4, 1941	Starts new career as radio broadcaster for St. Louis
Sept. 28, 1947	Makes last major league appearance as a pitcher for St. Louis Browns
1950	Becomes New York Yankees TV announcer
1952	Film Biography, "The Pride of St. Louis," released
1953	Elected to Baseball Hall of Fame
1955-1965	Announces for CBS-TV "Game of the Week"
July 17, 1974	Dizzy Dean dies in Reno, Nevada

JAY HANNA (DIZZY) DEAN
ST. LOUIS (N.L.) 1932-1937
CHICAGO (N.L.) 1938-1941

ONE OF FOUR N.L. PITCHERS TO WIN 30 OR
MORE GAMES UNDER MODERN REGULATIONS.
PITCHED IN 1934 (ST.L.) 1938 (CHICAGO)
WORLD SERIES. LED LEAGUE IN STRIKEOUTS
1932-33-34-35. SINGLE GAME RECORD WITH
17, JULY 30, 1933. FIRST PITCHER TO MAKE
TWO HITS IN ONE INNING IN WORLD SERIES.
MOST VALUABLE N.L. PLAYER IN 1934.

MAJOR LEAGUE STATISTICS

St. Louis Cardinals, Chicago Cubs, St. Louis Browns

YEAR	TEAM	W	L	PCT	ERA	G	GS	CG	IP	H	BB	SO	SHO
1930	STL N	1	0	1.000	1.000	1	1	1	9	3	3	5	0
1932		18	15	.545	3.30	46	33	16	286	280	102	191	4
1933		20	18	.526	3.04	48	34	26	293	279	64	199	3
1934		30	7	.811	2.66	50	33	24	311.2	288	75	195	7
1935		28	12	.700	3.04	50	36	29	325.1	324	77	190	3
1936		24	13	.649	3.17	51	34	28	315	310	53	195	2
1937		13	10	.565	2.69	27	25	17	197.1	206	33	120	4
1938	CHI N	7	1	.875	1.81	13	10	3	74.2	63	8	22	1
1939		6	4	.600	3.36	19	13	7	96.1	98	17	27	2
1940		3	3	.500	5.17	10	9	3	54	68	20	18	0
1941		0	0	-	18.00	1	1	0	1	3	0	1	0
1947	STL A	0	0	-	0.00	1	1	0	4	3	1	0	
Totals		150	83	.644	3.02	317	230	154	1967.1	1925	453	1163	26
World Series (2 years)		2	2	.500	2.88	5	4	2	34.1	28	6	19	1
All-Star Games (4 years)		1	1	.500	2.70	4	2	0	10	10	5	10	0

FURTHER READING

Allen, Lee. *Dizzy Dean: His Story in Baseball.* New York: G.P. Putnam, 1967.

Broeg, Bob. *Super Stars of Baseball.* St. Louis, MO: The Sporting News, 1971.

Broeg, Bob and William J. Miller. *Baseball From a Different Angle.* South Bend, IN: Diamond Communications, 1988.

Durocher, Leo and Ed Linn. *Nice Guys Finish Last.* New York: Simon & Schuster, 1975.

Einstein, Charles, ed. *The Third Fireside Book of Baseball.* New York: Simon & Schuster, 1968.

Fleming, G.H. *The Dizziest Season.* New York: William Morrow, 1984.

Greenberg, Hank and Ira Berkow. *Hank Greenberg, The Story of My Life.* New York: Times Books, 1989.

Pilner, Murray. *Branch Rickey, A Biography.* New York: Atheneum, 1982.

Smith, Curt. *America's Dizzy Dean.* Minneapolis, MN: The Bethany Press, 1978.

Smith, Curt. *Voices of the Game.* South Bend, IN: Diamond Communications, 1987.

Smith, Robert. *The Gashouse Gang, the Deans and Other Heroes.* New York: Simon & Schuster, 1962.

Williams, Joe. *The Joe Williams Baseball Reader.* Chapel Hill, NC: Algonquin Books, 1989.

INDEX

ICTURE CREDITS

P/Wide World Photos: pp. 2, 8, 18, 24, 29, 36, 40, 55; From the Collection of James Charlton: p. 46; Hake's Americana & Collectibles,
ırk, PA: p. 38; Movie Star News: p. 56; National Baseball Library, Cooperstown, NY: pp. 12, 15, 20, 23, 32, 34, 39, 42, 45, 47, 49,
2, 58, 60; UPI/Bettmann Newsphotos: pp. 26, 30, 31, 50

JACK KAVANAGH, a free-lance writer of sports stories, began writing about sports as a high school correspondent for the *Brooklyn Eagle* in the 1930s. He has been a contributing editor to *Sports History* and his writing has appeared in various magazines, including *Sports Heritage*, *Vine Line* and *Diversions*. His work is included in *The Ball Players*, *Total Baseball* and other baseball anthologies. Mr. Kavanagh lives in North Kingston, Rhode Island.

JIM MURRAY, veteran sports columnist of the *Los Angeles Times*, is one of America's most acclaimed writers. He has been named "America's Best Sportswriter" by the National Association of Sportscasters and Sportswriters 14 times, was awarded the Red Smith Award, and was twice winner of the National Headliner Award. In addition, he was awarded the J. G. Taylor Spink Award in 1987 for "meritorious contributions to baseball writing." With this award came his 1988 induction into the National Baseball Hall of Fame in Cooperstown, New York.

EARL WEAVER is the winningest manager in Baltimore Orioles history by a wide margin. He compiled 1,480 victories in his 17 years at the helm. After managing eight different minor league teams, he was given the chance to lead the Orioles in 1968. Under his leadership the Orioles finished lower than second place in the American League East only four times in 17 years. One of only 12 managers in big league history to have managed in four or more World Series, Earl was named Manager of the Year in 1979. The popular Weaver had his number 5 retired in 1982, joining Brooks Robinson, Frank Robinson, and Jim Palmer, whose numbers were retired previously. Earl Weaver continues his association with the professional baseball scene by writing, broadcasting, and coaching.